About the Author

I have always had a passion for storytelling, especially poetry, that evokes emotion and mystery, often engaging all the senses. I began to write micropoetry with mindful connections, a few years ago, and embarked on a wonderful journey, creating my own style that's led me to write this book. With a background in mental wellbeing and academic training, I have gained further knowledge of the power of the written word, especially micropoetry. Much of my work relates to thoughts and observations; reflections of my personal journey of self-discovery; gaining inner strength; and in some ways helping me make sense of my own life experiences. My story so far…

Soul Whispers
Micropoetry For the Pockets of Your Heart

Jan Smith

Soul Whispers
Micropoetry For the Pockets of Your Heart

Olympia Publishers
London

www.olympiapublishers.com

OLYMPIA PAPERBACK EDITION

A CIP catalogue record for this title is
available from the British Library.

ISBN: 978-1-78830-385-9

First Published in 2019

Olympia Publishers
60 Cannon Street
London
EC4N 6NP
Printed in Great Britain

Dedication

For Nancy x

Acknowledgements

For all those who believed in me from the start, and encouraged me throughout this journey, I am forever in your debt.

And for you, the reader, picking up my pocket poetry, my heart is full of gratitude.

Introduction

Micropoetry, expressing emotions that can often touch our hearts and souls.

Storytelling in a condensed form; evoking and engaging all the senses.

Much of my writings are reflections, thoughts and observations through academic learning, work based experience and my personal journey of self-discovery. Themes covered express our links with nature; resilience and mindfulness; self-awareness and inner strength; and cultivating aspects of kindness and compassion towards each other, and indeed ourselves. And poems of love with deep soul connections, full of ancient, mystical and celestial verses.

In this postmodern age, I believe these are such powerful subjects close to many hearts. I envisage this pocket poetry book to provide easy access and reference, with poems to enjoy and relate to. As with any poetry of prose, there is always individual meaning as each of our stories and experiences are unique to us; for myself, writing poetry has helped me to find my own purpose in life, strengthening my resolve and general wellbeing.

I do hope there will be a shared passion that brings us together, makes us feel alive, tapping into the many joys and mysteries of life, as well as the difficulties and struggles we may encounter. Helping us find new ways of being, as we fill the pockets of our hearts with words that may provide support, strengthen us from within, bring a sense of cohesion, in a time when many of us feel lost, even separate, from the wider community; an infinite creative and inspirational source we can connect to through a love of poetry, and by doing so, help reveal our authentic selves and true potential, our own precious contribution to the world.

Celebrate With Poetry

Celebrate
Why Does She Write Poetry?
Spilling Words
Into The Mystery
Poetess

Soul Connections

Stardust Souls
Celestial Love
Ancient Love Affair
No Clocks…
Dark Side Of Their Souls
Our Thirsty Hearts
The Way They Dance
Black And White?
Two Beautiful Souls
Softly Burn
His Morning Kiss…
Deep Red Thread
Come Sit With Me Awhile
An Illusion?
Where They Once Danced
Heart Whispers
Storytellers
Ardent Flamed Kisses
When…
Out Of The Blue
Their Forever Love

Oneness with Nature and The Universe

Slow Dance With The Stars
The Sweetest Crown
Our True Light
Spilling Her Story
Enchanting Song
Echoes Of Her Soul
Flow Of Life
Rhythm Of The Universe
Begin
Ancient Roots
Freedom
Gold And Evergreen
Connecting To The Stars
Ancient Planets Greet
Gentle Ebb & Flow
Strength In Her Heart
Autumn Colours Fade
Nothing Stays

Self-Discovery and Inner Strength

True Self
Am I Not Enough?
Autumn
Time To Let Go…
Majestic Dance
Authentic Self
It's Your Dance
Rediscovering Herself
Love Is All Around Her
Go Within…
Ordinary Moments
Your Soul Will Guide You
Dear Laura…

Resilience and Mindfulness

Standing Firm
Resilience
Begin Again
Her Fiery Soul
Fears And Thorns
Unlearning
Solitude
Breathe…
Go To Her…
Rhythm Of You
The Here And Now
Hope
A Sense Of Calm

Loving-Kindness, Compassion for Self and Others

Cultivate Love
A Sacred Space
Simplicity
Loving-Kindness
A New Kindness
Silent Blessings
Nature's Garden
Inner Light
Life Changes

Celebrate with Poetry

Celebrate

With poetry she nurtures her soul
Feeling her way through hope &
trembling loss alike
Spilling her words
Celebrating the recreation
of herself

Why Does She Write Poetry?

Because it makes her feel alive…
Transports her to far off lands
where she's free
Mystical places, way beyond
the horizon
Running through dark enchanted woods
And dancing with you in the moonlight
among the brightest
stars that just won't behave

Spilling Words

Writing poetry
Heartfelt & soulful
Spilling words
from the dusty
corners of her mind
Letting go of fear,
smoothing sharp
edges of her being

Into The Mystery

She feels poetry
pouring through her pores
pain, pleasure, fear & love…
It's all deep inside her bones & blood
To be alive she must go once more
into the mystery of life…

Poetess

She feels so alive today
Much like springtime at her fingertips
Words falling like petals in the breeze
From the sweetest delicate new bouquet

Soul Connections

Stardust Souls

Ancient roots
weave through many lifetimes
Those eyes full of new light
& flickers of yesterday
Two stardust souls finding home
Their forever hearts reunited...

Celestial Love

Chambers of her heart
full of passion
As dark as night
With his ardent flamed kisses
he scorched upon her soul
Their love story from the stars

Ancient Love Affair

Ancient love affair
Warriors in battle
A golden field of
fear & dreams
Where once their
blood was spilt
And on that day
they forged their
hearts together
for all eternity

No Clocks...

No clocks
No time
Just you & I
For love is infinite
between those
like us
with stardust souls

Dark Side of Their Souls

Sharing ancient stories
Intertwined
They're cosmic lovers
With storms & fire deep inside
Together the dark side of their
celestial souls
begin to shine like tiny diamonds

Our Thirsty Hearts

Lean into me
Real close
Shake loose those fears
Write with me
on the crumpled pages
of our lives
Drink, taste sweet wine
from our once thirsty hearts

The Way They Dance

He seems to know her
her thoughts, just a little bit more
than anyone else
Something about the way they dance
In natural rhythm with divine & immortal light

Black And White?

Not sure if in black and white?
But she saw him through the mist
& atmosphere
A memory of time gone by?
His silhouette smart, classy
like an old fashioned movie star

Two Beautiful Souls

Two beautiful souls connect
They dance in shadows
And fall in love in light
Their sacred place
An ancient haven
Where 'magic' comes to life

Softly Burn

When worlds collide
The universe begins to whisper
sweet words of wonder
Sparks fly, ignite
& two blossoming souls
so very softly burn

His Morning Kiss...

She wants his morning kiss
& his night-time romantic gaze
To drink his words
with autumn wine
Ruby red thoughts
of their eternal love

Deep Red Thread

Two souls
Oh how autumn holds
their dreams so tightly
Entwined in golden light
& deep red thread
that can never ever be broken

Come Sit with Me Awhile

Rest your soul
Come sit with me
in this safe haven
If you are tired
we don't need to speak
Silence brings its own rewards
I don't wish to talk about tomorrow
or try to change a thing
Just you and I
letting life flow
In this precious moment
come sit with me awhile…

An Illusion?

She's not quite sure
If this is a memory or an illusion?
But she believes he stole her breath
& her heart that summer evening…

Where They Once Danced

Light gradually fades
& memories appear
Casting form in dark corners…
Shadows of where they once danced
Endless souls entwined
They shared red wine passionate kisses
In a sultry & fragrant night

Heart Whispers

It's always about the soul
Doesn't matter about the past
And all that didn't serve you
Let this go…
Time to go within, listen to the whispers
of your heart, what do they say?

Storytellers

We are storytellers
Weaving magic
Casting light & shade through poetry
Come bring your book
& sit awhile
Let your words
soothe my soul once more
Each story helping to smooth
my deepest scars & sharpest edges

Ardent Flamed Kisses

Chambers of her heart
full of passion
as dark as night
With his ardent flamed kiss
he scorched upon her soul
their love story from the stars...

When...

When she can see deep inside your soul
& her heart rhythm is one with yours...
When she finds light inside the darkest
corners of your mind
& she can soothe your very being
with her sweet & tender touch...
She is love, your eternal love

Out of The Blue

Those special souls that come
at times out of the blue
Who enhance our lives
& feed our very beings
Shining light & hope
Keep them tucked
deep inside your heart pockets
To stay forever & a day...

Their Forever Love

Their forever love
Two beautiful souls entwined
since the beginning of time
Hearts woven together
by celestial thread
A thread of eternal love
that can never be broken
By time, or any twist of fate...

Oneness with Nature and The Universe

Slow Dance With The Stars

When the moon is low
She tilts her head
& gazes at the night sky
Falling deeply in love
with the slow dance of the stars…

The Sweetest Crown

Summer adorns the sweetest crown
Curls wrap around a daisy chain
She weaves wildflowers
through her long flowing hair
Such a sweet & delicate bouquet
Dancing barefoot in a meadow
full of gold
Summer colours delight of lilac
& yellow grace such a perfect day

Our True Light

Only when we begin to realise
our souls are a thousand years old
Can we cast our true light
onto the dark side of the moon

Spilling Her Story

Spilling her story
Writing words across the sky
Dancing among stars
& vast glittering moondust
Moving slowly to the rhapsody
that is deep inside her soul

Enchanting Song

Tucked away underneath nature's umbrella
Listening to the whispers of mother earth
Through the trees & wilderness you can hear
The enchanting song of her ancient soul

Echoes Of Her Soul

In touch with the echoes of her soul
Connecting to nature
& the natural rhythm
of her own beating heart

Flow of Life

Like the great oak tree
Deep roots of creation
Nature's energy
to soothe & heal
The flow of life
rising through her soul
A thrilling crescendo
Spilling over her very being
back into the earth below

Rhythm of The Universe

Create your own unique dance
Let your sacred spirit soar
& feel the rhythm of the universe
pulsate deep inside your heart

Begin...

Begin...
Unlearn all that has been your unspoken 'truth'
for as long as you remember
Breathe in new air filled only with love
Cast aside those fears, dear heart
that have kept you in a cage of doubt
Fling open the door of change
& fly with... Wings

Ancient Roots

Look inside her heart
Feel the pull of ancient strings
Each chamber entwined
with unconditional love
Connecting her very being
to the entire universe

Freedom

No walls
No barriers…
Just you & I…
Dancing under
the same stars
with the whole
world inside
of us

Gold and Evergreen

Wrap a golden cloak
around her gentle heart
Wildflowers will always
grace her path
An autumn bouquet cascades
of red, gold & evergreen

Connecting to The Stars

Storms come
blow through her veins
Soft skin wet
her tangled windswept days
She can taste the thunder
Dancing in the chaos
Connecting to the stars

Ancient Planets Greet

Take my hand
Let's go where a million
stars collide &
ancient planets greet us
We can dance, under the moon
& fall deeply in love once more

Gentle Ebb & Flow

Like souls rising through early morning mist
The gentle ebb & flow of the vast lake
Mountains standing, watching over, proud & still
Nature's heart so beautiful
reflected blue on endless ripples
The boats course across the water
creating white waves
lapping at the rocks
Laughter breaks tranquillity
Morning at the lake…

Strength In Her Heart

Strength in her heart
forged through endless time
Many treasures from
deep within
She stays humble,
into the mystery
falling into the vastness
Rattling the stars
Straight back up she gets
with fire in her soul

Autumn Colours Fade

Autumn colours fade
Seeds cast unseen
Through the darkness
Still into her garden she goes…
Letting go of old ways
Fears & thorns
Remembering sweet life is
Always just a dandelion bouquet

Nothing Stays

Her hair tangles in the gentle breeze
A little fresher is this wind of change
Butterflies near their final dance
Delicate nature, nothing stays
But the sweetest late summertime memories

Self-Discovery and Inner Strength

True Self

Her path turns
She cannot see
what's ahead
Yet is not afraid
to lose sight
of her unfolding soul
Trusting in her true
authentic 'self'
begins to set her free...

Am I Not Enough?

Am I not enough?
Do all spaces need to be filled?
The fallacy of what life should be,
just an illusion
For my soul knows just how to sing

Autumn

A time to scatter seeds of change
The gentle kind that feeds your soul
Pull out harsh weed, unwanted thoughts
that once tangled with your hopes &
sweetest dreams...

Time To Let Go...

She picked up
All the beautiful
fragrant wildflowers
And let go of all
the fears & thorns
that once weighed her down...

Majestic Dance

Don't lock your heart away
Let old ways go, be gone…
Cast old ways of being
to the winds
Fill your soul with hope
& joy
Fall back into love
& learn that majestic dance
once more

Authentic Self

Go within
Go deep, stay…
Beneath the ebb & flow of YOU
Feel the gentle rhythm of your
genuine self
Time to dance & celebrate all that you are

It's Your Dance

It's your dance
No need to explain
Feel your way between
the shadows
Through the chaos & tempest
Taste thunder, smell the last drops of rain
Fall, fall in love with mystery...

Rediscovering Herself

She lets life in
The touch of nature
Gentle breeze on her skin
Evoking all senses
Rediscovering herself
She begins to hear
heart whispers
from deep within her soul

Love Is All Around Her

She is love
It's all around her
Through her flaws & fragile bones
Beauty of her scars
Bruised knees & tangled dreams
Still, love is all around her

Go Within...

On the darkest of days
Go within...
There's an essence of pure light
A light so pure, so bright
it will illuminate a path to guide you
and touch so many hearts

Ordinary Moments

She finds much magic & mystery
in the most ordinary moments
Seeing all of life's beauty
through the lens of her
eternal soul

Your Soul Will Guide You

Even if you sink into dark shadows
& your heart feels heavy
Hope is still casting light nearby…
Listen, your soul will always guide you

Dear Laura...

Go at your own pace
Be gentle with your heart...
Tend to the beautiful roses
already in your garden
Thorns leave marks & scars,
but that's okay dear Laura
They make you who you
are today

Resilience and Mindfulness

Standing Firm

She stood firm
The storm came
it shook her bones
& left havoc at her feet
Tangled, heart racing
swirling air caught each breath
She swayed & wavered
but did not fall
She stood firm...

Resilience

The ebb & flow of things
Life brings so many storms
& sometimes throws you
against the rocks
Wild winds take your breath
& tangle up your dreams
Sway, buckle, bend
but you will not break
Salty sea will heal your wounds
The sun will come & kiss your skin
as the storm passes through

Begin Again...

She put down her heavy basket
Filled with dust & yesterday
Opened up her window
& let Autumn's breeze flow in
She picked fresh flowers from her garden
placed them on the table & began again...

Her Fiery Soul

Her fiery soul ignites
Of all the storms that have passed
and all that's yet to come
Throw what you will against the rocks
With true resilience she may falter
yet her endless spirit rebounding

Fears and Thorns

She picked up all the beautiful
fragrant wildflowers
And let go of all the fears & thorns
that once weighed her down
No longer to entwine in
her everyday bouquet

Unlearning

Sometimes you curl up
Stay in silence for a while
and that's okay
Let life wash over you
almost like unlearning
Releasing of all that
brings doubt & trepidation
to your door

Solitude

Away from disapproval
The drama & negative vibes
She's in her safe haven
Her own paradise within
with all she needs right now
Candlelight to guide her
Sweet poetry by her side

Breathe…

Let your brokenness heal…
Yet never forget the scars
& broken dreams
The hue & cry of life
teach us so much
& lead us ever nearer home…

Go To Her...

She's resilient, bold
Wears her golden heart
on her angel sleeve
Go to her...
You will find her
Off the beaten track
Near the flowing stream
In a field of white daisies
& a canopy of green

Rhythm Of You

That space between each breath
Brings a sense of calm, & healing
Go within
Drop below the surface
Become aware of the rhythm of life
Rhythm of you...

The Here And Now

Fall in love with the here & now
The uncertainties of life…
Dance in the darkness as well as light
Let shadows dance around our souls
There's much magic there, & light
will always be close by…

Hope

Even if you sink into the shadows
& your heart is heavy
Hope is still casting light nearby...
Listen to the whispers from your soul
they will always guide you...

A Sense Of Calm

Winds whistle through
leaving behind a force of chaos
Yet the storm will pass
& all that rages will fall flat
A sense of calm will appear
to soothe & heal those lost souls
Much hope is on the horizon
dear heart, all is not lost...

Loving-Kindness, Compassion for Self and Others

Cultivate Love

Cultivate love
The kind of loving kindness
that connects us all
Simple & seamless
random acts of kindness
& compassion can help
us all to grow & heal...

A Sacred Space

Kindness can fill dark corners
Just as candlelight casts flickers of hope
to form a sacred space
Where fear no longer hides
& the radiance of who we really are
Our truest nature may begin to shine

Simplicity

She longs for simplicity
Slowly clearing away
All that she has gathered
But is not…
Filling her open arms with self care
Scattering only seeds of love, hope
& authenticity

Loving-Kindness

Loving-kindness into her being
her every pore
Until her skin glistens like gold
Her parched mouth now refreshed
A sacred heart begins to gently heal

With A New Kindness

She lets life in now, with a new kindness
Self love
Through the touch of nature
& gentle breeze on her skin
Finally realising who she's meant to be
Heart whispers guiding softly
From deep within her soul...

Silent Blessings

Give silent blessings
with an open heart to all
Especially for those
who at this moment
Their fortune is less than ours...
This silent blessing
make this a daily practice...

Nature's Garden

When tending nature's garden
do not spend your precious time
feeding new soil with any traces
of fear or resentment
Sow only seeds of compassion
Tend daily with care
& watch it grow into an open space
filled with healing & kindness

Inner Light

Let your inner light guide you
Listen to the gentle wise whispers
from deep within your soul
Breathe, feel the shift towards self love
The key to all loving kindness
always begins with you...

Life Changes...

Life changes, keep on a path of self love
Remember what once made your heart sing?
The gentle rhythm of unlearning...
Slowly fall back into love with
your own unique, true self